FUNNY MONEY

FUNNY MONEY

Rosemary Burr

ROSTERS LTD

© Rosemary Burr and Rosters

ISBN: 0-948032-17-0

Published by Rosters Ltd
60 Welbeck St
London, W1

Printed and bound by Cox & Wyman Ltd, Reading
Typeset by Gwynne Printers Ltd, Hurstpierpoint, Sussex

This book is sold subject to the condition that it shall not, by way of trade or otherwise, be lent, re-sold, hired out or otherwise circulated without the publisher's prior consent in any form of binding or cover other than that in which it is published and without a similar condition being imposed on the subsequent purchaser.

All rights reserved. No part of this book may be reproduced or transmitted by any means without prior permission.

PREFACE

Welcome to the second edition of Funny Money. The first edition was written in the summer of '87 prior to the crash and saw the light of day a few weeks after that momentous collapse in stock markets around the world which left investors reeling.

Is it safe to go back to the typewriter I ask myself? Well, you the reader can be the judge. Watch out for movements in the FTSE 100 Index around the middle of October.

This edition has been extended to include the comments and reactions of the money men in the light of the crash of '87. Two new chapters have been added: "Crash, Bang and Codswallop" and the "Protection Racket". My thanks to Nick Kochan for his contribution to the second edition.

INTRODUCTION:
The World of 'Invisibles'

It's a funny thing about money, nobody likes to talk about the subject. It has become the last taboo. The rich keep quiet for fear of drawing themselves to the attention of the taxman or the burglars; the poor keep quiet for fear of attracting the bailiffs or worse the helpful old biddy from the consumers association round the corner. We talk about the earnings generated by our financial sector as 'invisible', even when they are the only thing which keeps the country in the black.

In the same vein, people who give financial advice can never bring themselves to utter those good old fashioned Anglo Saxon words 'buy' or 'sell' – instead they hedge their remarks in a strange code. This can make it virtually impossible for the ordinary person to understand a word they are saying, which may or may not be their intention.

This book tries to take the lid off the world of high – and low – finance. To provide you with a helpful phrase book when travelling in the strange and sometimes fantastical world of Big Money. To introduce you to the type of characters you will meet and their chief pursuits. Well, their one chief pursuit in many guises – getting their hands on your cash.

CONTENTS

Chapter One: The Magic of OPM 11

The bouncer. Confessions of a credit card junkie. Credit card fraud. Getting a loan. Safe as houses. The bank teller. Holiday money. Financial advice. Long term lending. Paying back the loan. Don't call us, we'll call you.

Chapter Two: The Invisible Policy 29

The claims proof policy. Settling the claim. Stories policyholders tell. Insurance salesman. Health insurance. Have policy, will travel. Life assurance. No surrender. Pensions.

Chapter Three: Claims People Make . 43

Accidental damage. Motorcar madness. Bank banana skins.

Chapter Four: Money Talks 51

Financial advice. Unit trusts. Insurance products. Homing in. Banking brief. Household bills.

Chapter Five: Bargain Basement 71

Privatisation. Great bores of our time. Getting a listing. Share option schemes. Shareholders perks. Takeover mania.

Chapter Six: The Good Old Days 89

Railway boom. Share sickness. Tip, tap. On the menu. From A-Z. Lot of bottle. Seconds out.

Chapter Seven: Gentleman and Players   105

Accountant. Actuary. Banker. Credit controller. Insurance broker. Stockbroker. Financial PR. The fund manager. The marketing team. The back office staff. Post Big Bang. The watchdogs.

Chapter Eight: Your Money in Their Hands 117

Great rip-offs. Investment game. The share con. The commodity scam. The company you keep. Cracking the media code. Portfolio planning.

Chapter Nine: Crash, Bang and Codswallop 135

Culture clash. Crash of '87. Local heroes. Crash landing. Reporting back.

Chapter Ten: Protection Racket 149

Rules of the game. Cloud on the horizon. Rumbling on. Consulting. Parting is such sweet sorrow. BP: when the gushing stopped.

CHAPTER ONE:
The Magic of OPM

'Perhaps it's the pie in the city sky that my financial adviser told me about'

How's this for a get rich quick scheme. You persuade people to hand over their cash, don't pay them a penny for it and only let them have it back in small amounts at any one time. Sounds too good to be true you may think. Well this particular scam is known as the 'current account'.

You need only look at the profits made by our big five high street banks to see that the quickest way to make money is with 'OPM' – other people's money.

Now the trouble with all super scams is that you can't fool all the people all the time. So the banks had to come up with a new version, scam two 'current account with interest'. OK, they argued if the people want interest, they can have it – but at a price. The price is something innocuously called bank charges, which magically disappear off the credit side of your bank balance without you even feeling the pain of signing a cheque or standing order.

The bouncer

A word about bank charges – the high street clearers really have this down to a fine art. You the poor unsuspecting customer pay a cheque into your account. It is made out to you, signed and correctly dated. Unfortunately it bounces – now not only do you end up without the cash, but to add insult to injury, your bank charges you a fee because the cheque bounced.

"Good morning – how much will it cost me if I open an account with you?"

Bouncing cheques are great business for banks. The person who wrote the cheque will be charged once for having it bounce and then charged again for the letter which tells him or her the cheque bounced. Then the person who did not receive the money may be charged several times. Most banks will re-present the cheque, i.e. try to get it paid up to three times. So you can end up with three charges – and still no money.

By the way there is a special law which only holds inside the four walls of a bank – it is 'we never make mistakes'. If you ring up to complain about the fact they cannot even spell your name correctly, they say it is 'the computers fault'. Bank computers it seems, by some gigantic leap of technological innovation, actually program themselves.

Confessions of a credit card junkie

Mr X is no fool. He too knows the value of OPM. Back in the 1970's he received a brown envelope in the post. To his amazement on opening the said envelope a little piece of plastic with his name printed on it dropped into his lap. It was called a credit card and could be used to run up bills in hundreds of shops. Mr X was hooked. He began collecting these pieces of plastic.

In those early days Mr X managed to fend off disaster by simply acquiring one new credit

card every few months. Everywhere he went shopkeepers thrust forms into his hand, he filled them in and miraculously six weeks later **another** brown envelope plopped through his door containing **another** piece of plastic.

Then a real breakthrough came. A letter saying he could obtain cash by placing his credit card in the cash dispenser and tapping out a few numbers. The cash could then be paid into his bank account and used to pay last month's credit card statement.

Mr X has now built up a record of paying off ever increasing debts and as such is highly regarded as a potential customer by the new companies in the credit field. Everyone it seems wants to lend him money.

The prognosis for Mr X is not good. The Bank of England recently pointed out to the banks that far too many people were using BM – the bank's money, when the banks should

"I bet my DAD'S OVERDRAFT can beat your DAD'S OVERDRAFT"

be using CM – the customer's money. This seemed to come as a complete shock to the banks, each of which never thought it might be sharing its customers with the rival down the street.

The banks are now thinking about putting their computers together and pooling credit information about their customers. The only trouble is – this takes money. So the poor old customer will end up with higher bank charges because the bank has been giving their money to people who can't pay it back.

The bank gets to make a profit twice – on the original loan and on the bank charges to its customers for checking out their credentials.

Credit card fraud

Sales assistants are carefully briefed to try and prevent thieves from using stolen credit cards. They are told to check that the name and title fit the description of the cardholder. The following tales have become part of credit card folklore:

- a six foot man, with brown eyes and a thick mop of dark hair speaking with an Irish accent was caught in Bristol using a card in the name of Wa Ho Fung

- an eighteen year old school boy was caught using the card of Lieutenant Colonel Jones when his moustache fell off at the counter.

Over in the United States they have introduced card holder's photographs in a bid to halt the crime wave, does it work? One thief put the picture of a gorilla on the card he had manufactured and used it fourteen times without being stopped. There is no documentary evidence of the state of his own physical appearance.

Getting a loan

As we have seen, banks make their money by lending out **your** cash to someone else – and, in theory, being repaid with interest. They have this strange view that lending to individuals is more risky than lending to governments. Countries they argue do not disappear. The countries may not, but their leaders and the bank's cash can – as they have discovered to their – I mean to their customers' cost – in Latin America and some parts of the Far East.

Of course, banks don't like to admit they have made mistakes – so they often lend these countries more money so they can pay the interest on these loans, even though they know the loan itself will never be repaid. This is called 'refinancing' or 'rescheduling' in the trade, and a bad debt by the rest of us.

The rescheduling game can only carry on until one of the participants – normally the borrower – breaches the rules and admits in public they cannot afford to pay off the original

*"Although my door is always open
MR GILCHRIST my mind is always closed..."*

loan – and making it bigger means they will never, never be able to pay off the debt.

We then move to a new game, called 'Write Off'. Here the banks simply say they will forget about the loan altogether provided, of course, the country remains a customer and takes out a new loan. They then put up their bank charges to make up the profit shortfall.

Safe as houses

Banks like lending people loans against the value of their homes, almost as much as they enjoy giving millions of pounds to foreigners thousands of miles away. So much so that sometimes they don't even check that the house will be owned by the person who wants the loan.

This leads to a new game, called Property Boom. Customers use BM, bank money to buy houses, which they then sell to other bank customers, also using BM, for a higher price. They then borrow even more money from the bank to buy a second house. The bank is quite happy as its original loan is repaid and then the customer borrows more. The customer is happy as he or she is using OPM to buy their home and making a profit. The taxman is unhappy as he cannot get his hands on any of the profits.

The game works fine as long as there are plenty of new players and not too many new houses. The trouble is the sight of all this profit

"Darling, do you think we will ever be able to afford FREE BANKING?"

quickly attracts the developer, who builds lots and lots of houses – bringing the whole game to an untimely end.

The bank teller

Handing customers their own money back is not something banks like to do. The bank teller therefore:

- never smiles

- is always busy doing important things when you want to cash a cheque

- always asks you 'how do you want it' – in the vain hope you'll take clothing coupons

- rations you to £50, however, much money you have in your account

- disappears for hours leaving the counter unattended

Special excuses – or, why you can never find a bank teller when you need one

Nat West: working for the action bank is so tiring I can't manage to hand a few quid across the counter

Midland: I hear what you say, you don't expect me to do anything as well

Barclays: sorry must dash, the eagle has flown

Lloyds: not available, gone to see a man about a horse

TSB: I've said 'yes', now I'm off for my lunch break

Not surprisingly customers will go to almost any lengths to avoid the confrontation with the bank teller. You can see long queues outside the bank branch in front of the cash dispenser even in the pouring rain. The advantages of

the cash dispenser are: it does not give you a withering glance, it does not say 'you again' and it allows you double rations per day.

Holiday money

The genius who invented the current account must have been reincarnated years later in time to create the traveller's cheques. This takes the principle of OPM to brand new heights. The bank charges you for the privilege of handing over your money – and then charges you again when you want to spend it. Also, if you buy traveller's cheques in a foreign currency it will charge you for the cost of changing your pounds into pesetas, drachmas or whatever. By the time you've bought your traveller's cheques you can probably no longer afford the holiday – and what's more the bank has the use of your money free and gratis until you cash the cheque.

Financial advice

Once you have given the bank your money they are loath to see it disappear from their coffers. The latest wheeze is called 'investment'. If you have a large bank balance they will suggest you could be earning more if you invested it in one of their products. Translated this means **they** could be earning more.

Here is how it works. Your money is on

"That's the trouble with the HONG KONG DOLLAR, an hour or so after using up your supply you feel like spending some more..."

deposit earning you a small amount of interest and the bank a big amount of interest. You are told if you put it in something called a 'unit trust' your money will grow. What you are rarely told is that the bank's share of your money will grow too. They will take £5 out of every £100 and add it to their profits. They will also charge you an annual fee.

Then, they will tell you the 'investment' is a long term matter so you should not even consider withdrawing your money for years and years. This way the bank gets its hands on your cash for a long time and you pay them twice.

This is known as 'BUTTING' in the trade, i.e. moving customers' money from bank balances to unit trusts. It is easier to perform South of Watford and virtually impossible West of Cardiff.

Long term lending

Banks don't like this. The more often they can lend out the same money the better, especially when it comes to large corporate loans. This is because not only do they charge their customers interest but something called an administrative fee. The more administrative fees they charge the better. Harold Wilson uncovered this game plan back in the 1970's but his report was so long that few bank customers could spare the time to read it.

"We're giving this free 'T'-shirt to all our new young investors"

Paying back the loan

This should never be attempted early. Banks just hate the idea of letting you off the hook. Many of them will actively discourage such perverse behaviour by charging you a fee if you wish to repay earlier.

Don't call us, we'll call you

Banks don't like to see their customers. They only call you in when they wish to see you. If all their customers turned up on their doorsteps they would not know what to do.

Indeed, banks got so concerned about the prospect of actually meeting their customers face to face a few years ago that they started closing down their branches. This had the added advantage that they could sell their branches at a profit to shops and building societies, who have not yet learnt the lesson that if you don't see the customer they cannot complain – and any mistakes can be blamed on the new computer in some offshore island.

CHAPTER TWO:
The Invisible Policy

*'I specialise in contractual small print and
large out-of-court settlements'*

While the banks get to look after mega bucks, the insurance companies do quite nicely in a rather more sedate way. The trick here is to get people to give you money, preferably monthly for life, and never pay them a penny back. Here's how it works. First you devise a policy to protect people from some horrible event, let's say their home being burgled. Then you work out all the likely circumstances, especially the most common, and word the policy so that if any of these run-of-the-mill events occur you don't have to pay the claim.

Reasons for not paying on a household contents insurance policy:

- you didn't turn your home into Fort Knox

- you go out to work leaving the residence unattended

- you fed the Doberman

- the fuse went on the rotating light dimmer

- the au pair gave her boyfriend the key

- you went on holiday for more than five weeks.

The claims proof policy
In other words insurance policies are written in what is called 'everything but' language.

"We offer a good salary and pleasant working conditions plus a company car when you die..."

This policy covers you against everything but . . . all the crucial escape clauses are in the small print.

If they don't catch you that way, the insurance companies have a real ace up their sleeves, it's called a 'material fact'. What's a material fact you may ask and quite rightly. It's a fact which the insurance company reckons you should have told it when you completed the form but as you did not, your policy is not valid.

When you complete an application form begging the insurance company to please, please take your money in return for insuring your home, goods etc., there is this sneaky little clause asking you to declare any material facts which may affect your request. If in doubt tell, they always advise. Some people have been known to add their life history in a desperate bid to nail the insurance company down.

Settling the claim

If the insurance company cannot use the material fact angle to wriggle out of settling a claim they can always fall back on the Penny Pincer Movement – PPM. First, they make you pay up part of the cost yourself. This for some absurd reason is known as the excess – probably because it makes policyholders put in a claim in excess of the real amount. Then there's the claims department who seem to use the same department stores as The Price Is Right – where do they find such bargains? They will trim down your demand for cash by apparently using a 1970's price scale for the discount store in some faraway shopping centre.

Stories policyholders tell

Mind you it would help your case if you could tell the insurance company, if not a consistent story, at least a feasible one. The number of UFO sightings on motorways and country lanes there have been, it's surprising we have not been taken over by the Martians years ago.

Here's some of my favourite causes of so-called accidents:

- the moving tree

- the phantom truck

- the strobe traffic light

- the dyslexic roundabut

- the other driver.

The insurance salesman

He – it is still mainly men – is a salesman with a mission. He is primed with facts and figures which would enable him to sell a home

"Let me through – I'm a PRIVATE HEALTH INSURANCE salesman"

contents policy to a squatter. In short, he is armed and highly dangerous to your bank balance. His genuine belief in the creed of insurance is given away by the fixed stare with which he tries to pin down his potential victims. All conversations are one track – and that track leads inexorably to you signing a cheque for the first monthly premium.

How to handle a hyperactive salesman:

- never dispute the value of insurance

- tell him you have heard all about the wonderful company he works for

- tell him you would have leapt at the opportunity to buy his policy but he was pipped at the post by the salesman from another firm

- suggest he talk to your dear friend and give him the appropriate name and address.

This latter ploy is a great way of dealing with any old scores you wish to settle.

Health insurance

This as its name suggests insures you against getting sick. Permanent Health Insurance insures you against being ill for a very long time. To buy this type of policy you first need to show that you are not sick – this is done by having a medical – and then, that you are not likely to get sick in future – this means filling in a detailed exposé of your sex life for the past eight or so years.

Have policy, will travel

This is designed to pay out if you are unable to travel or if you are robbed while abroad. It will not cover:

• cancelling your holiday because Roger, who turned out to be a female hamster, is having twins

• swopping holiday locations to avoid the office sneak

• deciding to stay at home and enjoy the freak heat wave

• changing your mind after reading 'The Stress of Holidays' by a leading US psychologist.

"The worry of whether or not he'll be able to keep his BUPA payments up is making RODNEY quite ill . . ."

Life assurance

The insurance companies are on a sticky wicket here. They pay people called actuaries vast sums of money to tell them what we all know anyway, that sooner or later everyone dies. So the companies have to devise ways of making you pay as much as possible for as long as possible. These include:

- index-linking your policy to the rise in Brazilian retail prices

- sending you a copy of the 'Joy of Chastity'

- dispatching vitamin tablets with your renewal notice

and last, but not least,

- forwarding you a list of hospitals with the shortest waiting lists.

NB: If you give up smoking, drinking and sex you may be able to reduce the cost of your life assurance. Whether you live longer will be a moot point – but it will certainly feel longer.

People are so loathe to buy life assurance, that the companies now try to look as if they are giving it away. They advertise savings plans with 'free' life cover, which translated means your money is divided between commission to our salesman, fees to head office, your life assurance premium and what is left will go into

a ten year savings plan. By the end of ten years they hope your money will have grown so much you won't notice the amount that was knocked off in the first place.

One of the best ways insurance companies have discovered to sell life assurance is to home buyers. This works on the sound psychological principle of hitting people when they are down. As anyone who has bought a home will know, there is this terrible sinking feeling that you will never be out of debt. That is when the clever insurance salesman pops up, waves a magic wand and shows you a way to turn those dreary monthly repayments into a fortune – in the year 2000 – by which time it will cost a fortune just to buy the groceries. And so thousands of endowment mortgages are signed each year and the insurance company gets richer and the bank, building society or salesman who arranged the policy gets richer – and you get bigger bills.

With a bit of luck in ten year's time you will be given a large lump sum, but by then you will have probably moved house at least once and need another policy to pay for your new property.

No surrender

You can tell how anxious the insurance companies are to keep your cash if you ask for it back, they call it 'surrendering' your policy. Surrender is not a popular word in an insurance salesman's vocabulary. He will do his damnedest to stop you taking the fatal step of withdrawing you cash. If you try this feat in the first few years of taking out your policy, he will look at you sadly, explaining that as you won't even get back the money you put in – it's hardly worth while. If really pressed he'll even offer to PAY YOU money not to stop paying them. This is called using your policy as collateral in the jargon or saving the salesman's skin in the vernacular.

Pensions

Insurance companies get a real kick out of selling these – once they have got your money they know they do not have to repay you until you retire. What's more thanks to the government's desire to encourage us all to pour our money into private pensions they can charge really large fees and still claim they are investing more than 100% of your money as they obtain rebates from the taxman. This tax

"Congratulations on joining the Staff Pension Scheme – or as we prefer to call it, our 'PAY NOW, LIVE LATER' fund . . ."

concession is so large that pension fund managers can sit back, relax and still beat their competitors flogging other investment products who are paying money to the taxman . . . which is going straight back to the companies investing your pension money.

CHAPTER THREE:
Claims People Make

If ever we needed proof that true life was stranger than fiction a trip to the claims office of any major insurance company would supply the evidence. The following examples are based on actual claims.

Accidental damage

Here's two examples of domestic strife:

> "I fancied my sister-in-law like mad for ages. Finally, after the Christmas party I made a pass at her. She kicked me in the groin – hard, and I've been off work for two weeks."

They say human beings look similar to their pets, do they I wonder pass on their habits as well:

> "A parrot was taught how to strike matches as a party trick. Unfortunately he did not know when to stop and managed to set light to the sofa."

Well, that's what was on the claims form.

"Bad news I'm afraid Madam. Your 24-piece dinner set is now a 48-piece dinner set . . ."

Motorcar madness

- Coming home I drove into the wrong house and collided with a tree I don't have.

- The other car collided with mine, without giving warning of its intention.

- I thought my window was down, but I found out it was up when I put my head through it.

- I collided with a stationary truck coming the other way.

- A truck backed through my windshield into my wife's face.

- A pedestrian hit me and went under my car.

- The guy was all over the road. I had to swerve a number of times before I hit him.

- I pulled away from the side of the road, glanced at my mother-in-law and headed over the embankment.

- I had been shopping for plants all day and was on my way home. As I reached an intersection a hedge sprang up, obscuring my vision and I did not see the other car.

- I had been driving for 40 years when I fell asleep at the wheel and had an accident.

"We also offer SYMPATHY . . ."

- I was on my way to the doctor with rear end trouble when my universal joint gave way causing me to have an accident.

- As I approached the intersection a sign suddenly appeared in a place where no stop sign had ever appeared before. I was unable to stop in time to avoid the accident.

- To avoid hitting the bumper of the car in front I struck the pedestrian.

- My car was legally parked as it backed into the other vehicle.

- An invisible car came out of nowhere, struck my car and vanished.

- I told the police that I was not injured, but on removing my hat found that I had a fractured skull.

- I was sure the old fellow would never make it to the other side of the road when I struck him.

- The pedestrian had no idea which direction to run, so I ran over him.

- I saw a slow moving, sad faced old gentleman as he bounced off the roof of my car.

- The indirect cause of the accident was a little guy in a small car with a big mouth.

"The bank next door says you've got all the money . . ."

- I was thrown from my car as it left the road. I was later found in a ditch by some stray cows.

- The telephone pole was approaching. I was attempting to swerve out of the way when I struck the front end.

Bank banana skins

When you open a bank account, you will be asked for proof of identity and references to show you are an honourable, upright and decent citizen worthy of a chequebook and cheque guarantee card. The following story tells of an applicant who seems to have got more than just his cheques crossed:

> "this man walked into the bank and asked if he could open an account. I said "yes", did he have some proof of identity and papers to show he lived where he said he did. Quick as a flash, he flourished a summons at me. This did indeed show his name and address – but also that he was accused of stealing from the bank down the road."

CHAPTER FOUR:
Money Talks

'If you want a good run for your money, go for gold'

One of the oldest sales tricks in the world is to develop a fast patter full of lengthy complex words which the potential customer is too ashamed to admit he or she does not understand. The following is a brief guide to surviving in the money world.

Financial advice

'tax consultant'
insurance salesman.

'investment adviser'
insurance salesman.

'independent investment adviser'
salesman for more than one insurance company.

'free advice'
you get charged for it anyway, so you may as well take it.

Unit trusts

'unique opportunity'
we've just launched the 2,000 unit trust in the country which is pretty much like hundreds of others.

'an award winning investment team'
our marketing director gave this journalist on one of the magazines a good lunch so we were named investment team of the year.

"I keep telling you MARION, I'm a Financial Consultant not a FORTUNE TELLER – it's not the same thing at all . . ."

'a sound investment track record'
we shoved all our stock market winners into this tiny fund and made sure it came number one in its sector for three months.

'unit trusts should be considered a long term investment'
we take 5% of your money straight away, so it takes us a little while to make this up.

'switching discounts'
usually when you switch your money from one of our funds to another we swipe another 7% of your money but as we have already taken 5% first time round, we will only take another 4% this time. This is called a 3% discount.

'the price of units may go up or down'
forget about all the sales pitch in large type we really have no idea whether we will ever be able to give you your money back.

'the fund will invest in special situations which offer above average opportunity for profit'
we are going to buy shares in small companies where we can make sure the price goes up.

'the fund will invest in smaller companies which have above average growth prospects'
we are going to buy shares in small companies where we can make sure the price goes up.

'the fund will invest in large, well established companies'
we cannot afford to pay the going rate for a

"Personally I've never been able to save enough to earn anything . . ."

brilliant fund manager so we are using a set of darts and the list of top 100 companies in the country.

'the fund is designed for income investors'
we are not sure we can pick shares which will go up in price but we can create income by buying a few government stocks.

'now is the right time to invest'
we had this idea nine months ago and we have finally got approval from the authorities to launch it today. OR, nobody has invested in this trust for ages, sooner or later it must go up in price, so buy now.

'your chance to share in the world's largest stock market'
we can't think of any sound investment reasons for buying American shares.

'your chance to share in the world's fastest growing market'
we can't think of any sound investment reasons for buying Japanese stocks.

'your chance to share in the world's emerging stock markets'
where the hell is Borneo on the map?

'a balanced portfolio to give you a secure spread of investments'
we don't know which stock market will do well so we are hedging our bets.

'an international fund'
we don't know which stock market will do well so we are going to put a little bit of your money in each and keep our fingers crossed.

'The Trusty American Fund'
a fund which invests in US stocks.

'The Trusty American Opportunities Fund'
the fund we launched when the American fund became too large for us to be able to manipulate the price.

'The Trusty American Emerging Companies Fund'
the fund we launched when everybody was bored with the other two.

'The Flamingo Trust'
the name we gave to our Far East Trust so we could put the pictures the chairman took on his holiday on the front cover.

'The Wessex Trust'
a special fund to invest in companies based in the development area of Wessex.

'The Happy Trust'
we don't invest in anything that goes bang or is made North of Watford.

'the fund will include holdings in unquoted investments'
if all else fails, we can show a profit by making up the prices of the unquoted companies whose shares we have bought.

'the fund's adviser will be a leading local firm'
none of our fund managers know the first thing about this trust. OR, it was cheaper to hire foreigners than take on extra staff.

Insurance products

'guaranteed income bond'
we've done our sums and worked out if we pay you a fixed income for the next five years we are guaranteed to make a profit.

'guaranteed bond from offshore insurer'
we guarantee to repay you your money if there is any cash in the kitty after the boss has bought his Caribbean home, the art treasures of the Western world and paid the divorce settlement for his third wife.

'tax free lump sum'
as in 'you'll enjoy the fruits of your policy free of tax' – we've already paid the taxman his whack so you don't need to pay him again.

'a unit linked policy'
another way we can flog units in our unit trusts, see 'a unique investment opportunity' on p. 52.

'your first three month's premiums entirely free'
we have just put up the annual cost by 50% so we can afford to reduce your charge by a third and still make a profit.

"*I'm afraid you don't understand Sir – your MORTGAGE PROTECTION POLICY doesn't protect you from US . . .*"

'no salesman will call'
we will send round our executive investment consultant.

'an all risk policy'
this policy covers all risks except the ten pages of exclusions and any items of real value.

'no claims discount'
a way to stop you making a claim on your motor insurance.

'valuable'
something you have to pay extra to insure.

Homing in

'estate agent'
someone who puts their feet up in other people's houses and practices writing fiction in the office.

'bijou residence'
too small to swing a cat.

'modern decorations'
the previous owner went in for splatter painting the walls.

'within easy walking distance of the tube'
marathon runners can get there in twenty minutes. OR, the living room shakes every half hour as trains rattle underneath.

"Sometimes these loft conversions just don't work"

'ideal for young childen'
next door to the local borstal.

'good parking facilities'
the neighbouring house does not keep a car and will rent you their garage space for a fee to be negotiated.

'in need of redecoration'
dilapidated.

'quick sale'
has been on the market for nearly a year.

'owners going abroad so prepared to reduce the price'
has been on the market for almost a year.

'valuation report'
something you pay for but never see and which determines whether or not you will get your mortgage.

'valuation and survey report'
something you pay a bit more for than an ordinary valuation report but do get to see. However you cannot rely on it to show up all the structural faults – for that you need to buy a full structural survey which is very expensive.

'housebuyer'
someone who seems more interested in the contents of your cupboards than the structure of the building.

Phrases people use when they are not interested in buying:

● what a lovely home you have

● I must ask my husband/boyfriend/wife/girlfriend first

● did you know your floorboards squeak if a twenty stone lady jumps up and down on them

● how many times has this block of flats featured on Crimewatch UK?

● why is the building covered in scaffolding?

"We could stuff our cavity walls with these heat conservation leaflets . . ."

Phrases people use when they are interested in buying your house:

- will you take part payment in cash?

- can we value the fixtures and fittings at £20,000?

- are you planning to take the dishwasher with you?

- what number do you wash your whites on?

- does the porter prefer whisky or gin?

- we've just seen our dream home and IT was £5,000 cheaper.

Banking brief

'free banking'
you get free cheques, standing orders and direct debits as long as we have lots of your money and don't pay you any interest. The bank charges you would have paid are billed to customers who go overdrawn.

'clearing cheques'
the way banks get their hands on your money for at least one day without paying you interest.

'credit card'
a way banks can charge stores a flat fee of up to 4% in return for permitting the stores to give you one month's credit.

'bank statement'
something which shows you how much the bank has taken from your account.

'bank branch'
somewhere which is closed when you need it.

'credit insurance'
something the banks like you to buy so if you cannot afford to repay the loan the insurance company will do so instead.

'cash'
something banks would rather not handle. If you pay in large amounts of notes and coins

"Had a terrible weekend – played golf with my bank manager and won . . ."

they will charge you a handling fee. If you want to draw out large amounts of cash you have to give them twenty-four hours warning.

'foreign currency tariff'
the notice displayed on the bank counter showing how much it would cost you to buy a variety of foreign currencies if the bank had them in stock.

'cheque guarantee card'
a means of rationing your cash withdrawals.

'cash dispensers'
machines which forget how to dispense cash on weekends.

Household bills

'budgeting'
something other people do.

'bills'
liners for the kitchen drawers.

'... or else letters'
the ones which need to be paid.

'household expenses'
bills which defy gravity.

'telephone bills'
first, there's a charge for NOT using the phone

payable in advance and known as a standing charge. Then there's a charge for using the phone. They no longer send final reminders so it's easy for the less efficient to get cut off. They then charge you for cutting you off and putting you back on again – and you still pay the standing charge over the period when you are cut off.

CHAPTER FIVE:
Bargain Basement

'A posse from the fraud squad have rounded-up a gang of stock market cowboys'

For some reason shrouded in history share deals are referred to as bargains, perhaps the phrase was coined by an eighteenth century wag with a perverse sense of humour. Here's some more phrases to help you feel at home in the world of stocks and shares.

'a bit of bully'
buying a few hundred pounds worth of oil exploration shares in the hope they will rise in price.

'stag night'
when the speculators celebrate their rich pickings from the newest government issue.

'bearing up'
trying to cope with falling share prices without resorting to leaping from the nearest rooftop.

'striking a bargain'
accepting the price you are given.

'rights issue'
the right to cough up more money.

'stock from a bucket shop'
the dregs.

'Rampo'
the stock exchange Rambo who can push up prices higher and faster than any other person.

'puff the Magic Dragon'
recommending Hong Kong stocks.

'spreading the risk'
a term coined by market makers buying stock at 15% less than you would sell it.

Privatisation

This is a really clever way of cashing in on OPM. The government sells the public shares in companies which they already own – what's more it uses their money to persuade them to buy the stock. However, everybody is happy: the government gets its cash, the company may get some extra money, small investors sell out for a profit and large investors can look clever as they have made paper profits.

To join the privatisation bandwagon you require:

- a newspaper from which to cut out the application form.

- a pen to fill in the form.

- a cheque – there's not often any need to have cash in your account as you won't be holding on to the shares for long.

- a stamped and addressed envelope

and, the really difficult bit,

- an old fashioned pin, to attach the cheque to the form.

Basic knowledge of the three Rs – reading, riting and rithmetic – is required to fill in the form but you'll even get lessons on television to help you.

The people who make really big money from these privatisation issues are not surprisingly those who handle your money. The share dealers who buy and sell your stock sometimes make almost as much profit as the small investor.

Great bores of our time

If you think men talking about football is boring then try dropping into your local pub in the midst of privatisation mania. There you will find:

- The BT bore

He has made one profit out of the stockmarket and still regales you with tales of his acumen and derry-daring years later.

- The crashing bore

He lost all his money in the stock market crash of 1974, spends his time cadging drinks off everybody else and predicting gloomy tidings.

- The bore on the telephone

The pub owner who is trying to ring up enough charges to offset against his British Telecom vouchers.

'Perhaps we should consider joining the share-owning majority'

- The nudge and a wink bore

He has just bought a share whose price has dropped like a stone and is trying to persuade everyone else to invest to push the price up again. Then they'll think he's clever and he can get his money back.

- The loaded bore

He's too drunk and rich to realise no one is listening.

- The twelve bore

He has invested in the last twelve privatisation issues and can afford to pay for everybody's drink thus ensuring a good audience throughout the evening.

- The wild bore

He bought shares in the one privatisation issue which sunk like a stone, Enterprise Oil, in 1984, and chokes on his beer when he listens to how the rest of the regulars fared with BT.

- The portfolio bore

He only got half the message and is still hanging on to all the shares which everyone else has sold. Instead of stories about quick profits, he discusses the state of his portfolio, the chartist's theory and what his stockbroker said on the phone last week.

Getting a listing

The term listing is the technical expression for getting a company's shares quoted on the stock exchange. It is quite literally a licence to print money, i.e. share certificates in return for investors' cash. Before a company can be listed it has to produce a prospectus telling potential investors how great it is and explaining in some detail why they should hand over their cash.

Here's a sample of the type of prose you can expect in a prospectus:

Company: Domestic Recycling Utility.

Activity: acquiring old mattresses, stripping them down and recovering them for retail sale.

Profit record: profits doubled last year when the directors found a cache of gold coins in one of the mattresses and decided to stick them in the company kitty.

Potential profits: profits look set to double again – the directors can't find a fence for all the gold coins they have discovered for the past five years, so these too will be put in the company bank account.

Directors:
Mr X, aged thirty-three. Managing director. He has managed to fool the taxman for ten years.

"I suggest we adjourn for lunch – which reminds me – let's hope that in the coming year we have a lot more fingers in a lot more pies . . ."

Mr Y, twenty-eight years. Marketing director. He has an extensive network of ex-Borstal mates who he meets for a jar in the pub every Thursday.

Mr Z, aged forty. Sales director.
He drives the pick-up van.

Mrs X, aged twenty-two.
Wife number three, who acts as a tax deductible secretary.

Dividend prospects: the company intends to pay a small dividend of 3% per share in the first year. Thereafter dividends will depend upon its future performance. However, as a growth orientated company the directors expect to plough back most of the profits into the firm, i.e. their executive pension schemes.

Shareholders' benefits: the company will pick up free of charge any of your old mattresses and dispose of them at no cost to yourself.

The retail analysts at a leading firm of stockbrokers commented as follows:

> "Domestic Recycling utility is a niche company in a growing market area with no obvious competitors. Its shares are quoted in the highly fashionable sector, retailers, where price earnings ratios of 40 or more are not uncommon. The company looks set

to double its pre-tax profits each year for the next few years and should therefore be regarded as a growth stock.

Recommendation: buy for medium term growth."

With comments like this, as you would imagine the launch would be a big success and overnight Mr and Mrs X, Mr Y and Mr Z become paper millionaires. They do in fact declare doubled profits in the following year and the share price rises giving them a chance to sell part of their holdings at a handy profit. Since they are used to giving back handers they were pleasantly surprised that all they had to pay was a fee to the broker and their merchant bank to arrange all this. They therefore quite understood when after two years their broker suggested a rights issue – which would be a 'nice little earner for them both'.

Since the supply of old mattresses stuffed with money was fast running out they decided to use part of the cash to diversify. Their broker explained they should look for a business which had 'synergy' with their own – that meant anything they felt they could handle comfortably. Their broker also said that there were rumblings about the need for the board to be stiffened with some more experienced people who could cope with the company's expansion.

Mr X thought long and hard. Then he had a brainwave, Mr P ran an old junk shop in the local high street. He was fifty years old, so the right age to meet his broker's requirements, and while Mr X's staff were hulking mattresses they could just as soon be hulking old chest of drawers, tables, chairs, etc. as well.

Mr X's stockbroker was ecstatic at his client's quick grasp of the synergy concept. The shareholders were ecstatic about the chance to make more money from the new shares. Mr P was so ecstatic about becoming a millionaire he divorced his long standing wife and married Elsie, his shop assistant, who was only nineteen. And, of course, Mr and Mrs X, Mr Y and Mr Z were even more ecstatic – they upgraded the company cars, developed a recreational facility for their staff . . . of four, and put even more money into their executive pension fund.

The moral of this story is . . . never throw away an old mattress without ripping it apart first to see if any valuables are inside. Or, other people's money can make you a fortune if you know the right stockbroker.

Share option schemes

Not everyone is cut out to run their own business, so how do the directors of public companies where the shareholders are largely institutions make their killing on the stock market. In the old days it was quite easy – they used inside information to help them decide the best time to buy and sell shares.

This has now been made illegal, so they had to come up with an alternative. It's called a share option – it's a bit like betting after you know which horse has won the race.

Here's how it's done.

The directors decide among themselves that they would like to be able to buy shares in the company at today's price in say five years time. They wait five years, if the price has risen, they go to the company secretary and ask him to issue some shares specially for them at the old price ruling five years ago. Of course, if the share price has fallen they don't bother. Generally this is not good news for other shareholders as the directors sell these new shares for a quick profit which tends to push down the price of the company's shares.

Incidentally where you may wonder do the directors find the money to buy the shares in the first place. Of course, they use OPM, i.e. they borrow the money from the bank for the necessary few days. The bank makes a small profit, the share dealer makes a small profit, the directors make a big profit – and the poor loyal shareholders tend to lose out.

Shareholders' perks

These are designed to promote shareholder loyalty and develop camaraderie with the company. In fact, their main use is ensuring companies whose names would otherwise not

"JANE – let me introduct you to MR CHEETHAM, he's something in the FINANCE JUNGLE . . ."

grace the City pages with acres of press coverage each time there is an article on wider share ownership.

Takeover mania

This is generally good news for the shareholders of companies which have forgotten why they went into business in the first place and whose shares have accordingly languished during the great charge upwards to new price peaks. The moment a company's name is mentioned as a potential bid target its price rises making it more expensive for the purchaser. Indeed, the only way some companies can keep the predators at bay is to repeatedly deny they are in bid talks – nobody believes these denials and their share price rises anyway.

Takeovers are a prime example of the magic of OPM. The predator uses its shareholders' money to buy off the target company's shareholders. The merchant banks, share dealers and brokers get their usual fee. Everybody concerned spends a lot of effort in keeping the prices of both companies up as high as possible – the bidder so he needs fewer shares to buy the target company and the victim so he can get a better price for his own carcase.

This is a great game while the match is in full swing, but once the whistle blows and a winner is declared most of the fun is over. The

"Known in the business as FOLDING MONEY"

staff of the bidding company have to find something to do with their new acquisition – if only willing buyers for different bits of it. Their own share price tends to slink back with the speculators chasing new 'special situations' and the loyal shareholders tend to see their profits shrinking.

The only way to keep the share price up is to talk about another takeover or revert to the opposite strategy of denying anyone is going to bid for you. The latter course will provide the directors with a profitable escape route and dump the growing problem into the hands of a third company and its shareholders.

CHAPTER SIX:
The Good Old Days

'Personally I regard anything other than Alpha and Beta Stocks as Non-U'

The stock market mania we have witnessed in the last few years with investors literally battling to get their application for Rolls Royce or British Gas accepted has turned the doorways of some great British banks into fortresses worthy of Wapping. Desperate investors look poised to hurl themselves through plate glass doors if that is what it will take to get their application form accepted. To add insult to possible grievous bodily harm in a recent case some investors who had beat the deadline discovered later their forms were mouldering away in a sack in a forgotten corner of the bank – never even to be entered in the ballot.

Railway boom

The nineteenth century saw similar scenes of greed and panic as investors – even women – were drawn into the net of trying to make a quick profit out of the railway boom. This story which dates back to that time shows that even in those days it was often women who kept a firm hand on the purse strings:

> 'She was a lady given to dabbling in stocks, and, as a matter of course, was a mark for every promoter and swindler; but it will be seen from what follows that she knew her way about. One of the advertising men sent her a circular recommending a certain but very doubtful stock, remarking that it was

"My diagnosis MR PRENDERGAST is excessive WITHDRAWAL SYMPTOMS..."

"good enough to put her bottom dollar on". She erased the word "dollar" and sent the circular back.'

Punters were warned about being drawn into duff schemes designed to produce simply profits for their promoters rather than products for the people. Among the type of 'fly-by-night' investments the nineteenth century shareholder was warned against were 'extracting silver from lead, an air pump for the brain, curing the gout and stone' and finally, the ultimate fantasy, 'a flying machine'. Could they possibly have known about the 1974 oil crisis and Freddie Laker?

Share sickness

Despite this sound advice a large number of people it seemed succumbed to a terrible sort of share sickness. Its symptoms were:

> 'idleness and inattention to business, and a neglect of study; the patient leaving good books to read the newspaper supplements. As the disorder progresses, the conversation becomes wild and incoherent, and remarkably disagreeable to all sane hearers, by running continually on Shares, Scrip, Premium, and Grand Junctions.'

By this stage the victim cannot tell fact from fantasy and writes for shares in companies

"Count your blessings George"

which 'are and always will be, imaginary'. What's more he sells his home, business – all his worldly goods to feed this fantasy until he comes to a cold, lonely, bitter end 'his disorder is an unrecognised madness, his only asylum is the workhouse or the jail'.

Well, thankfully we don't have workhouses now, but this sorry tale of the punter who got his wires tangled through a touch of 'Railway mania' is a lesson to us all.

Tip, tap

There's a common saying in stock market circles, 'where there's a tip, there's a tap'. The following tale illustrates this saying:

A. 'I say old man, do you want to make some money?'
B. 'Rather. I'm on.'
A. 'Well, go and buy yourself ten Unified.

They part. A few days later on meeting again they discuss the fact the stock has fallen in price.

A. 'I'm awfully sorry about the tip I gave you the other day.'
B. Why? When you told me to buy myself ten, I immediately went and sold ten, and have just bought them back at a 2% profit.'

On the menu

Before Big Bang the stock market was quite

literally a place full of gossips and salesmen who would have graced the stalls at Covent Garden. Business was conducted in a flurry of hand waving, there was no time for lengthy discourses so a rich vein of stock market lingo developed.

Here's how the nineteenth century 'market makers' described their stock:

Ales
Allsopp & Sons ordinary stock

Apes
Atlantic 1st mortgage bonds

Ayrshires
Glasgow & South-Western Railway ordinary stock

Bags
Buenos Ayres Great Southern Railway ordinary stock

Beetles
Colorado United Mining Company shares

Berthas
London, Brighton & South Coast Railway deferred ordinary stock

Berwicks
North-Eastern Railway consolidated ordinary stock

Bones
Wickens, Pease & Co. shares

Bottles
Barrett's Brewery & Bottling Company

Brums
London & North-Western Railway ordinary stock

Bulgarian Atrocities
Varna & Rustchuk Railway 3% obligations

Caleys
Caledonian Railway ordinary stock

Claras
Caledonian Railway deferred ordinary stock

Chats
London, Chatham & Dover Railway

Chinas
Eastern Extension Telegraph shares

Cohens
Turks, 1869. (Now Group III)

Cottons
Confederate dollar bonds

Cream-jugs
Charkof-Krementschug Railway bonds

Dinahs
Edinburgh & Glasgow Railway ordinary stock

Dogs
Newfoundland Land Company shares

Doras
South-Eastern Railway deferred ordinary stock

Dovers
South-Eastern Railway ordinary stock

Ducks
Aylesbury Dairy Company shares

Haddocks
Great North of Scotland ordinary stock

Kisses
Hotchkiss Ordnance Company shares

Knackers
Harrison, Barber & Company shares

Leeds
Lancashire & Yorkshire Railway ordinary stock

Mails
Mexican Railway ordinary stock

Megs
Mexican Railway 1st preference stock

Matches
Bryant & May shares

Mets
Metropolitan Railway ordinary stock

Middies
Midland Railway ordinary stock

Muttons
Turks, 1873. (Now in Group III)

Noras
Great Northern Railway deferred ordinary stock

Nuts
Barcelona Tramway shares

Pots
North Staffordshire Railway ordinary stock

Pigtails
Chartered Bank of India, Australia & China

Roses
Buenos Ayres & Rosario Railway ordinary stock

Rollers
United States rolling stock

Sarahs
Manchester, Sheffield & Lincolnshire Railway deferred stock

Sardines
Royal Sardinian Railway shares

Shores
Lake Shore & Michigan Southern Railway shares

Souths
London & South-Western Railway shares

Stouts
Arthur Guinness, Son & Co. shares

Sunshades
Sunchales Extension of the Buenos Ayres & Rosario Railway Co. shares

Vestas
Railway Investment Company deferred stock

Virgins
Virginia New funded

Whip-sticks
Dunaberg & Witepsk Railway shares

Yorks
Great Northern Railway ordinary stock

From A-Z

They also had quite a poetic turn in those good old days. In between chasing beetles, dogs and ducks they came up with the following verses on stock market life:

THE STOCK EXCHANGE ALPHABET

A is our Architect, weighed with care.
B stands for Broker, for Bull, and for Bear.

C 's the Contango that's paid by the Bull.
D the Defaulter who can't pay in full.

E the Electric Light – always going out.
F the Financiers, who're never in doubt.

G for the cheese – Gorgonzola by name.
H for the House that is built of the same.

I the Investor, with good store of cash.
J is the Jobber, who cuts such a dash.

K are the Knowing ones – awfully clever.
L is the Limit, which cometh off never.

M are the Managers, stern, yet serene.
N are the Notice boards everywhere seen.

O is the Option to put or to call.
P is the Panic that causes a fall.

Q 's the Quotation the brokers require.
R are the Rates which rise higher and higher.

S Speculator, who stumbles along.
T is the 'good Tip' – invariably wrong!

U is the stock which we Unified call.
V the Valarium which hangs over all.

W for Wetenhall, famed for his list.
X is a letter I fear must be missed.

Y are the Yankees whose prices we get.
Z is the Zeal this is done with – you bet!

Lot of bottle

Stress and seeking consolation at the bottom of a glass were as rife then as now. This little story shows how you can spot market trends before you get hold of the next day's papers.

CAUSE AND EFFECT

'It is said that Mabey's barmaids always know how the markets are going. When things are very dull and markets are tumbling to pieces, a greater number of "nips" are taken, spirits being in great demand. On the other hand, when everything is going up, there is a general run on iced drinks, champagne, and other light beverages.

'They can always palm off a tough steak on a Bull in a rising market; but have to give a Bear something very light under the same circumstances. Bears are bad eaters, even when things are going the right way for them. Bulls eat tarts and buns, Bears drink spirits and leave the pastry alone.

'A Bull eats his dinner very quickly,

whereas a Bear eats slowly and grumbles about everything. Bulls are easily pleased; Bears want a lot of attention. A sharp waiter knows what a customer is, and treats him accordingly.'

Seconds out

While today's market makers sit grimly huddled over their screens, largely doing deals with each other by flicking a few switches, jobbers in the old days were not adverse to throwing a few punches at their competitors. Here's the reminiscence of an elderly gentleman back in the nineteenth century:

> "When I first came here the place was very different from what it is now. We were only a few hundred strong then, and everybody knew everybody else. I think the tone of the business is lower now. Of course, increased competition has had its inevitable effect. We used to deal at wider prices then, and commissions were paid in full. Bucket shops were not even looming in the future.
>
> We had some fine games in the old days. At 2, Capel Court, Mendoza had a boxing booth, where, instead of knocking prices about, a member could go and knock somebody about or get knocked about himself, if things did not suit him inside.
>
> An old woman had a stall *inside* the House, close to Capel Court door, where

those who had not quite outlived their earliest tastes could feed on buns, cakes, etc. She eventually, so it is said, made a small fortune out of the members, and retired from business. She had a moral reason for it too – she said the Stock Exchange 'was such a wicked place'.

A gallery ran round the old House; seats and desks were fitted up for clerks and members. It was very convenient, because if a man wanted a book he simply called up to his clerk, who would throw it over. Some of the funny ones used to drop things over on unsuspecting members.

Sometimes, in the afternoon, a jobber used to give us a tune on a cornet, and I reckon we had plenty of fun when things were dull. The whole character of the business has changed since then, and I fancy that if some of the old boys could come back again they would hardly know their own business.

We used to buy our own chops and steaks in those days, and take them to a cook-shop or chop-house and have them cooked, paying a penny for the privilege; they furnished the vegetables and drink, bread, etc. That is the origin of all the cooks at the chop-houses expecting a penny in the present day. The modern palatial dining-rooms were not even thought of."

What would this gentleman think about Amsterdam bucket shops mailing his customers or nouvelle cuisine served forty storeys up in a dining room suspended on thin air, bricks and mortar? As for commissions, the current level of fees structure with all those decimal points would hardly be considered worthy of the name.

Source: The quotes are taken from 'House Scraps: an entertaining look at Stock Exchange life' published by Rosters Ltd on behalf of Abbey Life Unit Trust Managers.

CHAPTER SEVEN:
Gentlemen and Players

*'For God's sake stifle the rumour John.
It will be a red rag to a bullish market!'*

Most of the people employed in managing our money are men, although a few women have discovered that there are well paid jobs in the City which require no manual labour – apart from an ability to wag your tongue. So what sort of people take home vast valaries in return for acting as financial baby-sitters?

- Accountant

Anybody can set up shop as an accountant, so this could be the yob from down the road or the yuppie from Eton. The main qualification is to be able to balance the books. This takes a lot more creative skill than most accountants are often given credit for – namely the ability to create items of expenditure which appear to have some relation to the company's business, rather than to the chairman's home in Antibes or his mistress in the Barbican.

- Actuary

These are the people who beaver away in the back office, number crunching statistical data and making projections based on current figures into the year 2000 and beyond. The main qualification is a total ability to disregard the present – they are always working on past data and making predictions about the future. It is a good profession for those with a cowardly streak as actuaries are unlikely to be around to witness their mistakes. An ability to get on with your fellow man is not required.

"I see you can't afford my fee"

- Banker

The main qualification here used to be an ability to add up but this is no longer required in our computerised age. A long nose to look down and glasses to peer over helps as does the dexterity to scrunch up your face like Phil Cool when in the vicinity of customers. Creative ability is not required at the outset but comes in handy later on when you are refusing the fiftieth application for credit in a single day. Being long sighted also helps because that way your judgement on potential loan applicants will not be clouded by their physical appearance.

- Credit controller

The ability to say 'no'.

- Insurance broker

The ability not to take 'no' for an answer.

- Stockbroker

In times of rising share prices, no ability at all. In times of falling share prices a clean driving licence so you can moonlight as a mini cab driver.

There are also a number of people who don't actually do anything but tell other money managers what to think. These are called research or share analysts. The main quality here is a tough constitution which will put up with endless company lunches and poor hearing so you will disregard the chairman's stories of how well the company will do next year. Also, the ability to double the number you first thought of when doing profit forecasts in a rising market and find another occupation in falling markets.

- Financial PR

The ability to take the chairman out, get him drunk and then keep the story about his exploits out of the papers. Great creative skill is required to build up the company's image. This involves getting the chairman photographed next to the best looking buxom blonde in the room and then leaking the story of his liaison to the popular press. This is called giving the shares a 'leg up'.

The fund managers

These are the people who do the REAL THING and invest your money. They need a fast line in innuendo to bring down the share prices of companies which their rival fund managers have bought. A good wrist action to throw the pin in the list of stocks, a strong sense of fantasy to interpret the curves in the share price graph and an endless source of optimism so that any company whose share price has fallen can be sincerely described as 'a recovery situation'.

An ability to speak Japanese and stick a pin in a list of stocks will guarantee you a job of

about £50,000 per year but you will be wheeled out to make the chairman look good on his annual visit to Tokyo. A weak bladder to justify frequent trips to the men's room where you can pick up tips from your mates in corporate finance is also useful.

Experience is not essential for fund managers. One marketing manager at a foreign bank was offered the job as an international fund manager for one group and has changed jobs every six months ever since. To date no one has discovered he still thinks a warrant is something issued by the police.

"The number of people showing an interest in my savings has increased by FIFTY PER CENT over the last two years . . ."

The marketing team

Strange as it may seem they need the ability to add up – that's because they tend to promote the fund which has risen the fastest in the last six months. Investment skills are a positive disadvantage as they are always arguing the case for funds which were top performers last year, rather than those which may do well in the future. If it has moved up, sell it – is their motto on fund promotion.

A certain creative talent is required to package the same product several times over and make it look different – but this is limited to being able to rearrange about a dozen words in different orders. The marketing manager's manual is '101 Ways To Use The Word Special'.

The back office staff

These are the men and women responsible for sending your policy via pigeon express to the person with the same name as yours who lives in the Outer Hebrides. The main technical skill required here is being able to jam the phones to avoid the incoming flood of complaints from customers who have not received the right bit of paper.

In the past before the explosion of interest in stocks and shares the back office was a quiet pleasant backwater where staff could disappear for years only to turn up to claim their gold watch. Now it has become a seething hot bed of activity and the staff need to be able to think up as many excuses as possible to explain why they still have not processed last week's orders. Since they have not had much practice in the art of excusing themselves they keep coming up with the same boring tale, namely that they 'did not expect to actually have to process **so much** paper'. They thought they could stare into their coffee cups and chat up their mates in personnel as they always had done in the past.

Post Big Bang

On October 27, 1986 the old guard bowed out of the City and left the field to the new breed, largely foreigners who really enjoy working for a living. Staff suddenly discovered they had to be clocked in and clocked out. What was worse, they were meant to work for a full eight hours rather than sneaking off to the pub for a five hour lunch.

You can tell this new breed of City gent by the following:

- the lack of an old school tie.

He bought his from the Tie Rack as he rushed off the red eye express.

- the glint in his eye.

This is not greed but he's still high from the cocaine he took to keep him working through the past five nights

"*As well as academic qualifications MR BOLSTRODE the position calls for certain physical attributes, NARROW ICY-BLUE EYES and RAZOR BLADE-THIN LIPS for example...*"

- a transatlantic accent.

This is either genuine, i.e. was acquired after a spell working on Wall Street, or fake, i.e. an attempt to fool the new owners into thinking he is 'one of them'

- a name tag.

So the new receptionist can recognise the slackers and report them to head office

- a title which includes the words vice president

- crumbs down his jacket.

To prove he had a sandwich lunch while sweating over his hot desk

- last year's suit.

To show he has not had time to buy a new one

- a wife who wears this year's fashion

To prove he is a rising executive

The watchdogs

With the passing of the Financial Services Act (1986) the City has to learn the lesson that it must be SEEN to be giving the small investor a fair deal. This has led to a whole host of new organisations and lots more jobs for the boys – especially those who cannot cope with the rough and tumble of life in their merchant banks or stockbroking firms since Big Bang.

The best job is compliance offer – you get to say 'no' to everyone from the office boy to the chairman when they ask whether they can do something. You can have hours of fun scrawling over documents with a big red pen and writing derogatory words in the margin. You can make people re-do perfectly acceptable work over and over again – all in the name of consumer protection. You can settle old scores in this way and nobody can refuse to do as you say.

If you are really skilled you can bring the whole organisation to a complete standstill in a matter of weeks and drive the senior staff to early retirement.

CHAPTER EIGHT:
Your Money in Their Hands

'There's a fool on the line who wants to be parted from his money'

If somebody stopped you in the street who you had never seen before in your life and said they would invest your money for you, would you give it to them? The answer is probably no, but put that same stranger in a fancy West End office and the answer for many people would change to 'yes'.

Great rip offs

a) the investment game

The financial conmen know that to make a real killing they have to invest a little bit of OPM in their business. Here is the way they do it. They set up a company in some far away offshore island where there is no corporation or income tax and, very important this, no extradition treaty with the UK or EEC.

Then they establish a branch in London and develop a few products, usually some sort of insurance bonds. They then hire a chauffeur driven limousine and go to Ascot. Here they find their first customers. So sure are they of their investment ability that they guarantee to repay these investors cash in six months, if they are not happy.

After six months, they tell their customers their money has doubled. Most are so happy they leave the money where it is, a few withdraw the cash to pay off their betting debts or estate duties. These are paid out of the other client's money. Both sets of customers tell their friends how well they have done.

"Put it this way – if you don't expire soon our life savings will . . ."

Customers rush through their doors, their Swiss bank account bulges and when they reckon they have milked the local populace dry they do a bunk with their fat bank balance and retire to the aforementioned offshore haven.

How to spot the game taking place:

- the office furniture will be new

- the secretary will be ugly – they are chosen for their reliability not their good looks

- they will move into new offices every six months

- they will have a motto about consumer protection on the wall

- they will have walls filled with charts showing lines go vertically upward

b) the share con

Really smart operators can kill two birds with one stone on their first visit to that aforesaid offshore haven of rampant capitalism. They set up a company, preferably one involved in exploration – anything that can justify asking people to cough up lots of money without expecting too quick a return. Then they write a prospectus which states the company has acquired the rights to look for gold in some

obscure Third World country. Shares in this little minefield can be sold by letter via a post box or on the phone to your 'investment' clients.

How to spot the share con:

● the letter will be franked in Amsterdam

● there will be a child's crayon map of the soil's subsection

● there will be a map of the world with a minute cross to mark the spot of the fictional mine

● there will be a chart showing what percentage of the mine has already been purchased

c) **the commodity scam**

To be strictly truthful you don't need to get

involved with conmen to lose your shirt in commodities, you can do that quite quickly and painfully enough without any help. The conman's trick is therefore to make you believe you lost money through commodity dealing when all the time he pocketed your cash.

How to spot the scam:

- you discover you have completed fifty deals in a day at prices no one in the market has witnessed for thirty years

- you sell oil futures when the Gulf war blows up

- you sell orange juice futures when Florida has its biggest freeze in history

- you made a small profit on your first go, but then lost when you invested a large sum. You made another profit when you hinted a millionaire friend of yours might invest if there really were profits to be made.

The company you keep

Many people have put their money into stocks and shares for the first time and are discovering the thrill of receiving that missive known as the report and accounts. Do not be deceived – this is designed to tell you as little as possible while giving you the minimum facts required.

"Capital punishment"

The terms 'facts' is, of course, used loosely.

Here is a brief introduction to the world of chairman's statements:

'underlying uncertainties'
we have no idea what is going on

'moving strongly ahead'
we may just make a bit more profit than last year

'the directors have decided to forgo a salary increase'
the directors have doubled their tax-free pension contributions and started a share option scheme

'difficult trading conditions are being experienced'
we are making a loss

'the outlook is favourable, providing nothing unforseen occurs'
we have no idea whether we will make a profit or loss

'solid progress is being maintained'
we may just be able to cook the figures to show a rise in profits

'increased competition is putting pressure on margins'
we are showing a loss

'margins are improving'
we are showing a smaller loss than last year

'abnormal trading conditions'
we are making a large loss

'the order book is strong'
the marketing director took out the sales director from our biggest customer, got him drunk and he agreed to double last year's order

'we shall seek to work hard to improve profitability'
we can't promise anything

'given the difficult conditions, the results are very satisfactory'
the board are quite happy and have voted themselves a pay rise, but there's not enough spare cash to increase the dividends for shareholders

'our growth in profits would be impossible without the loyalty of our staff and customers'
the only way we grew was by acquisition and if the people who know how to run these businesses leave, or their existing customers go elsewhere, we will be in trouble.

'while the underlying trend has been favourable, short term hicoughs in the widget sector has reduced profits'
we thought we were going great guns and then some fool in widgets threw a spanner into the works

'we will develop the profit potential of the widget division'
sales in the widget division have been lousy

'most of our profits are traditionally made in the second half of the year, so it is difficult to predict the outcome for the full year'
we are keeping our fingers crossed that the weather's not too bad this winter and people spend money in our stores

'your board plans to grow through acquisition'
we need to hide lack or organic growth

'we plan to strengthen your board'
one of my pals needs a job

'your directors believe a change of domicile would benefit the company'
the Fraud Squad are on to us

'we have broadened the base of the business'
we have stumbled across something we didn't know we owned

'we plan horizontal growth'
we can't spell perpendicular

'your board is set on a programme of diversification'
we're in the wrong business

'we have plans to expand abroad'
the chairman is fed up holidaying in Bournemouth

'we have introduced strict financial control'
we are running out of cash

'due to unforseen circumstances'
circumstances seen by everybody except the board

Cracking the media code

To keep on the inside track of your company's fortunes you will need to be able to crack the code of short hand terminology used by the financial press. While many people wrongly assume all journalists require several pints and plenty of imagination to write their stories – indeed I was once accused by an insurance salesman of writing an article while drunk on a train, presumably because it got nowhere fast, – in fact, financial writers choose their words with great care.

Lesson one: reading between the lines on company news

'glamour stock'
an overpriced share where the company has no assets

'fancy rating'
an overpriced share where the company has no assets and no prospects of earnings growth

'troubled'
loss-making

'controversial'
the Department of Trade and Industry is building up a file on this person/company

'high-flier'
the board think they've inherited the Midas touch

'agressive'
buys anything in sight

'not a company to take risks'
dreadfully boring, sell your shares

'restructuring'
the company's main business is making a loss, so it's going to try something new

'management buy-out'
last ditch attempt to flog off assets when there are no buyers

'dealing irregularities'
someone's been caught with their hand in the till

'possible breaches of the Companies Act'
someone important has been caught with their hand in the till

'board shake-up'
half the directors got sacked for making a mess of the business

'key director quits'
either, one director got sacked for making a mess of the business, or one director left because he thought the rest of the board was making a pig's breakfast of the business

'will take time to show through to the bottom line'
they will make a loss for the forseeable future

'under review'
the board has not made up its mind yet or the directors never thought about that issue until the journalists asked the question

'subject to market conditions'
if share prices are going through the roof

'according to anecdotal evidence'
what one market maker said after lunch/on the early morning train/in front of his secretary

'core business'
the bit the company cannot sell

Lesson Two: read the next section on portfolio planning.

Portfolio planning

Everyone it seems knows what YOU should do with your shares. The main hazard is working out what their advice means. Words such as buy, sell, profit and loss are completely taboo. Instead, you have to learn a new language and how to interpret the slightest mellowness in tone.

You'll find the phrases below creeping into journalists' reports on stock markets, your stockbroker's newsletter and even those smart portfolio managers who spend a lot of time talking about the 'internationalisation of global securities markets' which just means one stock market somewhere in the world, however obscure, must be going up.

'market sentiment'
what other people think

'bargain hunters'
buyers who are thin on the ground

'realising your profits'
sell your shares while the going is good

'the share price has suffered from speculation about losses'
the company is about to go bust, so all those in the know have sold their shares

'more to go for'
you were a mug not to buy the shares a week ago, but you might still make a profit if enough other mugs like you pile in now

'fully valued'
only a mug would buy at this level

'overvalued'
only a mug would hold onto his shares at this price. Or, the price is about to collapse

'volatility'
we don't know what on earth is going to happen next

"To stop money burning a hole in his pocket, HENRY spends it like WATER..."

'diversify your portfolio'
sell your shares and buy tins of food

'share prices are virtually unchanged due to the low volume of business'
the market makers are on holiday

'moving firmly ahead'
prices are rising slowly

'take-over activity is at a significant level which will improve market sentiment'
people are bidding for anything that moves, so the market makers are marking prices up right across the board

'this is a disappointing area'
this market has collapsed by 30% and the local brokers are committing suicide in droves

'a correction'
a fall in prices

'a short-term correction'
we are keeping our fingers crossed prices will stop falling soon

'the weight of money argument'
we can't think why this stockmarket should go up but other people are prepared to put their money in

'consolidation'
a fall in prices

'signs of incipient recovery'
we are keeping our fingers crossed that prices will start rising again

'major recovery'
thank goodness prices have stopped falling.

CHAPTER NINE:
Crash, Bang and Codswallop

"I was offered some free advice before the October crash, but it turned out to be worth nothing"

One of the beauties of Big Bang in 1986 was that for the first time banks could own stockbrokers and even jobbers. The Stock Exchange celebrated the new environment by letting off a huge number of balloons – hot air, perhaps. The 'for sale' signs went up outside many medium sized stockbrokers and the partners themselves studied the 'for sale' signs outside their dream mansions on the South coast. They waited for the offers of big bucks.

The offers came, foreigners and banks leapt on the securities bandwagon. It was the height of the roaring bull market. Government privatisations were in full swing. What was there to lose? The simple answer turned out to be money – literally millions of shareholders' cash.

Culture clash

Turning back to those heady days in 1986 – the bear market was hardly a glimpse in a clairvoyant's crystal ball. What was apparent was the dreaded CC – culture clash. An ex-partner of a firm of stockbrokers which had just been taken over by a bank was sent a memo by the personnel department. It said that in accordance with usual practice he would be given half a day's leave in the week before Christmas for Christmas shopping. His reply was as follows: "I'll be shooting every day in the week before Christmas, so I'll take it in-the-week-before-the-week before Christmas, thank you very much." (Courtesy of Fred Carr, erstwhile head of private client business at Capel-Cure Myers, now sold out to a foreign bank with a long name.)

A quote about another merger from an earlier period: "National Westminster is the love-child of two banks who merged in 1970 – did I hear rumours of 'You bastards'?"

The Crash of '87

The Crash of October 19, 1987 took everybody – well, almost everybody by surprise. For a start people were not quite sure what had happened. President Reagan tried to defuse the situation by suggesting it was a mere "correction" and one stockbroker later in the month gave his tips on television for "after all this nonsense is over".

Few people were in a position to gloat and say "I told you so". Perhaps the next best thing was John Davis in *The Observer* who said he would have told his readers but he was on holiday at the time. "It has saddened me that I was on holiday last weekend," he wrote, "and thus was not able to warn you of the dangers lying ahead for world stock markets."

Certainly the investors were well beaten. There was the obscure but fabulously wealthy American Warren Buffett. In the weeks before the crash, he bought into American investment bank, Salomon Brothers. An American

newspaper reported glowingly, "Buffett has an extraordinary record for spotting companies and sectors which are about to enjoy a major long-term revival. He is not the sort of man to buy into a brokerage house just before a great crash." In fact, he did just that.

In the global marketplace of London, some advanced the "it couldn't happen here" theory of stock market behaviour. A financial intermediary takes the wooden spoon. "We are telling clients not to panic. What happened, has happened in America. The UK will be sound." The market as we all know then went on to fall over a quarter, more than it ever fell in the great crash of 1929. So much for financial advice.

Before the crash, Robert Holmes a Court was Australia's richest man. He was said to be personally worth £500m, and his company, Bell Group, £3bn. Taking defeat was not easy. In November 1987 his press spokesman was reported as saying: "Contrary to rumours, Bell Group has a positive cashflow. Our only problem is to restore our credibility in the marketplace and in the media. We are in a war, but no boats have been sunk." The jokes at his expense were legion. For example:

Question: "What is the difference between Holmes à Court and a can of Fosters?"

Answer: "About 50 cents."

However, perhaps the London firm of brokers, Phillips and Drew knew what was coming when, a week before the crash they produced a desk-top computer which provided fund managers with a means of assessing the effects of economic shock on equity sectors.

There was not much humour around the City in those dark hours, but such as it was, was black. Stockbrokers would stare at their screens in wonder at the huge drops in the market. Said a boss to his junior "that's a record". His reply: "Sir, that's a golden album." What went wrong? Analysts groped around their charts for the answers but as another market wit commented: "In this market you don't need to be an investment analyst, you need to be a clinical psychologist."

When the markets were so volatile in those fateful days in October, every rumour became credible and ominous. At 11.37 am on Black Monday, October 19, a rumour swept the City – the US had invaded Iran. "That's all you need when everyone's nerves are shot to blazes," said a broker with a line in metaphors, "besides, knowing the Americans they'd probably miss Iran and hit Cairo."

Rumours about bankrupt American brokers flinging themselves from the top of skyscrapers turned out to be false. One supposed sighting of broker about to end it all turned out on closer investigations to be a routine window washing operation. Indeed, it seemed that the brokers had just as much to fear from their clients as vice a versa.

It was reported in an American paper that "a client got so mad with his stockbroker for losing his investments and life savings that he dressed up in a Santa Claus suit and kidnapped him from a Christmas party. He then took the broker to a cabin near the West Virginian border and tortured him for two weeks with a home made electric chair." Another even more aggrieved client shot two Merrill Lynch brokers after losing $8.2m in the crash.

In Britain, it seems the small matter of losses were sorted out, well, a little less violently. One senior broker was quoted after the crash as saying "there are bound to be some absolute stinkers, but there won't be many firms who won't pick up the tab for their losses".

Local heroes

Some of the biggest losers in Britain became national heroes. It was even reported that the trainee accountant at County NatWest who managed to accumulate losses of £1m on the traded options market was inundated with job offers.

A 15-year-old schoolboy also needed bailing out. The authorities found he had run up debts of tens of thousands of pounds. The headline to the newspaper story ran: "Danger of Dealing with the Under-Aged". His headmaster tried to steer clear of controversy by saying: "He is a very polite boy of average ability." Well, he certainly didn't spot the crash.

"My computer's speechless!"

Crash landing

Once the crash was out of the way, people could start to laugh again. Some wit advertised the Great Crash Commemorative Tie. A story came out of New York, the home of many of the best crash jokes, that a parrot had been discovered belonging to an investor who had gone bust in the crash. "More margin, more margin" it cried, echoing the cry of its lost owner who had been ruined trying to meet the margin of his stockbroker.

One stereotype American yuppie quipped: "Maybe we should call it 'Fall Street'." Even Woody Allen had something to contribute to the general dismay. He is reported as defining a stockbroker as "someone who invests your money until it is all gone."

In *The Times* there was a typically British stoical cartoon at the time: "good thing we diversified from shares to notes under the mattress" ran the caption. Not all crash jokes were in such good taste. There was a report that the only financial brightspots were markets like Ethiopia, where one dealer commented "What crash?" To which the logical reply was "What market?"

The crash, as we know, was truly global. An advertisement in an Australian newspaper ran: "Stockmarket crash sale. The stock market crashed on Tuesday. On Thursday the Porsche was sold. I am now offering my powerboat building business to the best c(r)ash offer in the next seven days."

After the deluge, markets tried to assess, and play down the effects of the experience. There was a bright side, a stockbroker's wife returned home looking relieved after a car accident, "what's the matter dear, have you crashed the car?" her husband asked. Her reply was: "it was not a crash, I merely corrected the position of the bumpers."

The UK stock market also tried to understand what had happened, and the result was all too familiar self-congratulation. Sir Nicholas Goodison's study of the crash: "The main finding is that our market worked rather well in that testing time. Let us be thankful that our market displayed in October a sturdiness and flexibility that enabled it to bend but not break in the great wind that blew."

One marketmaker on the stockmarket during the crash was not quite so sure: "When there was a market floor we just ran faster to carry out the bargains. Now we've got the computer which just packs up when it can't cope."

John Banham, the head of the Confederation of British Industry, climbed on the complacency bandwagon. He jetted into London from a holiday in early November, and said the crisis was over. He dismissed the "Jezebels in the City, and declared there was no crisis." However, the crash has been a disaster for the marketmakers, because it created a lack of confidence in the stockmarket and investors stayed away from dealing in shares. A story was revived from the last big crash, in 1974. Apparently, a mouse was espied on the floor of the Stock Exchange which one of the brokers was about to bash, when someone shouted out – "don't kill it, it might have an order!" A message from the *Sun* newspaper summed up the prevalent view: "Forget the stock market for now, Folks," said the headline in Sun Money.

Reporting back

Here's how some major companies told their shareholders about the impact of the crash.

- **BAT's 1986 report:**

"Strong growth and development in all our major business activities made 1986 an excellent year for the group. . . . It is most encouraging that the successful implementation of our declared strategies have won wider recognition in the stock market. By the end of the year, the company's market capitalisation had passed the £7 billion mark and more recently, in 1987, it reached £8 billion."

- **BAT's 1987 report:**

"The year 1987 was one of continuity in the group's strategic development. It was a substantial achievement to hold pretax profit almost unchanged despite the fall in the dollar and the decline in investment markets."

"I'm constantly reminding Muriel that being a City slicker isn't always a barrel of laughs"

The BAT's chairman does not gloat over the most recent post crash market capitalisation. It stood in July 1988 at a much reduced £6.28 billion.

- **BZW 1987**

For the first nine months of the year the securities trading market activity enjoyed significantly increased income. . . . Trading losses sustained principally in equity market-making as a result of the stock market decline gave rise to a loss of £11m for the year. Despite lower levels of market activity, BZW traded profitably in the final two months of the year.

- **NatWest Investment Bank 1986**

"1986 has been a stimulating first year. We have integrated three businesses with different cultures and traditions, we have recruited nearly a thousand new staff and have built up six new operations. The process of deregulation, de-intermediation and securitisation continues unabated on a global scale, creating unprecedented opportunities for new products and services."

- **NatWest in 1987**

"Events in the world stock markets had an adverse impact upon investment banking results for the year. That impact, taken with the cost of establishing a securities operation cost some £116 million."

In 1987, County NatWest made heavy and controversial redundancies.

- **Midland in 1987**

Earlier in the year, in March, we had come to the conclusion that the prospect of adequate profits was too remote to warrant the continued commitment of financial and human resources to this area. Subsequent events have convinced us that our decision was correct and led us to withdraw from UK institutional equities altogether.

- **Barclays in 1987**

The world background was in 1987 no more than favourable even before the drop in share prices. The outlook for 1988 is clouded by the events of Black Monday.

CHAPTER TEN:
Protection Racket

"The originators of this management agreement have bent the rules to suit themselves"

1988 was billed as the year of investor protection. Although the Financial Services Act was passed in 1986 it took a further two years of wrangling and mud slinging before it was partially implemented in April 1988. It seemed very much a case of both too little, too late and too much, too late depending on where you stand. For consumers who had hoped to rest secure under a blanket of protection with the ultimate safeguard of a compensation scheme it was rather galling to learn only the first £50,000 of their money *was protected* and that, if they happened to be ripped off in a busy year for rip offs, they could find their payments scaled down. For the companies whose activities are governed by the act it was definitely too much, too late. The authorities seemed to equate thoroughness with weight, the physical weight of the rulebooks.

There are plenty of facile jokes on the subject. For example: "What do you do when you have thoroughly read and understood the FSA. Do it again, as you cannot have read it properly."

The FSA is designed to regulate the money sharks and investment rogues. However, as one practitioner, Christopher Sharp of the Northern Building Society, nicely illustrates, corruption is always in someone else's backyard: "The verb to be regulated is conjugated, 'I am above reproach, you sail close to the wind, he has got to be banned'."

Regulation has meant a proliferation of new

initials. An advertisement for Britannia units trusts read "SIB, Fimbra, Lautro – is it all Greek to you?" Another wit, playing with the initials, (for names much, much too long, complicated and unimportant to spell out here), said: "Rolac, Lautro, Fimbra, Nasdim, Lutiro, SIB, Miboc; do not despair, DDT kills all these." One disgruntled practitioner summed up his frustration with the act by saying: "there is nothing wrong with the FSA that hanging three civil servants a week won't cure."

Rules of the game

From the customer's point of view the first visible sign of investor protection at work landed with a hefty thud on their doorsteps at the end of June. The envelope contained a client agreement, a legal document they had to sign before they could instruct their financial adviser to do any business. Most were clearly designed to protect the company from the investor. Gullible customers were asked to agree to:

- be woken up in the middle of the night with hot share tips
- buy shares in companies whose prices were artificially inflated
- have their share orders amassed with other punters, even if this meant paying a higher price
- pay exorbitant interest on any outstanding bills

- tell their life history in two pages

So much for an improved service.

Cloud on the horizon

No sooner had the new rules on investor protection come into force than the first major scandal of 1988 broke – Barlow Clowes was wound up by the Securities and Investment Board, the City watchdog. There's not much to laugh about when people's lifetime savings are dissipated – but the case did produce some classic statements of the "he would say that, wouldn't he? variety".

- Clowes' solicitor: "I don't have any doubt that Mr Clowes is an honest man. I don't think that the calibre of his business acumen can be seriously contested."
- A personal friend of Clowes: "You could not call Clowes a flash Harry, although he was definitely obsessed with the good life."
- "My primary interest is to safeguard the interest of investors" – Clowes shortly before he was arrested.

Perhaps the most appropos statment given that Barlow Clowes's gilt edged fund turned out to be invested in anything but gilt edged securities was the comment of a one-time director: "I know a gilt from an equity but basically I am a marketing man. Who am I, a Gibraltarian, to question the investment decisions of a magnate like Clowes?"

Rumbling on

Compared to the on-going Guiness scandal, Barlow Clowes is small beer in money terms. The true story of the derry-doings during Guiness's bid for Distillers will probably never emerge, but the comments of some of the chief players in the tragedy are illuminating:

- Former chairman, Ernest Saunders: "I am not a man versed in financial and City matters."
- Gerald Ronson's covering note when returning £5.8m to Guiness: "I had not focused on the legal implications."

Consulting

A new kind of securities analyst reared his head during the spate of takeovers. Hunchbacked men in the proverbial raincoats were discovered bugging people's houses. During one particularly hard fought bid there were rumoured to be so many security men on both sides that they spent the whole time tracking each other – leaving the key figures free to go about their business. One consultant really took the biscuit – his bugging device was found concealed in an old biscuit tin at the bottom of a telegraph pole outside the home of one of the target company's executives.

Parting is such sweet sorrow

All those yuppies who had been lured to the City by the aroma of mega bucks and huge

"Pssst! – Know of any job vacancies?"

commission cheques found there was little but air between them and the dole queue when the chips were down. Old hands who had weathered previous stock market squalls gained new status in organisations which operated the last in, first out policy. The term "boy" took on a new meaning – burnt out yuppie.

The yuppies found there was little to protect them from dismissal, although generous redundancy payments helped to take part of the sting away. If consumers sometimes feel that their financial affairs could be dealt with more quickly and efficiently, the same could not be said for those employees in the firing line. The speed with which they were sometimes literally removed from the premises and even barred from returning to their desk was something to behold.

One firm told its staff over the tannoy: "You and you, don't report for work." To make sure the named individuals didn't come back, they wiped out the smart cards used as a pass into the building.

At another stockbroking firm, the papers record that employees arrived at work only to learn that the axe had fallen. They were told to clear their desks and leave within hours. Said a spokesman, "it seems awfully cruel, but they have left today".

The generous redundancy payments did not always calm the angry young things who had had it so good, and one yuppie dealer who had just lost his job, took his Porsche, parked it

"Your smart card doesn't work anymore and neither do you"

across the entrance to his firm's carpark, locked it, and threw the keys into a drain.

A yet more disgruntled employee, was the 38-year-old, $400,000-a-year Wall Street merchant banker who on being sacked, went home to his newly wed wife, and said, "I suppose you'd like me to jump out the window?". Her reply, if any, is not known, but he went and did just that.

Companies have not always fared badly out of sackings. It sometimes turned out that their shares leapt when the market heard about the cost cutting involved. It was one of the few reasons left to the remaining analysts to support a bullish company report.

When a leading overseas bank sacked 120 from its stockbrokers, its press statement was particularly disingenuous: "It has nothing to do with the crash of October 19. This is something we have been working towards for a period of months. It's simply a question of bringing two organisations together."

A short-lived magazine, called *The City*, targeted at people earning over £40,000, carried in its first issue an article saying: "Mega-job-loss-tales reflect wishful thinking by jealous journalists, who have been fed their lines by miffed City elders." That was the only issue of the magazine, as its owners, Reed, closed it down, putting its editor out of a job.

"Your secretary says she's very sorry she forgot to send off your BP application form"

BP: when the gushing stopped

BP was billed as a popular privatisation issue, on a par with British Telecom, or British Gas. The national excitement mounted as small investors warmed to the idea of another massive premium when the shares were launched. There was a newspaper cartoon at the time, whose caption read: "One could almost hear the wife saying to her husband: 'have you turned the lights off, put the cat out, and filled in the application form, dear'?"

The press expressed the euphoria. An article in *The Times*, had the headline: "BP set for 30% premium", and the text read, "Demand from overseas is so strong that the premium price expected to be offered by Japanese and US buyers will compensate for the discounts being offered."

The government also got excited. Said a government minister Norman Lamont: "Share ownership in Britain is no longer a rich man's hobby. The government is hoping this sale will promote wider share ownership."

It was reported that over 6.25m individuals had registered with the Share Information Office, and NatWest was expecting "record breaking business" for its share-dealing service for small investors when trading in BP shares started. On Tuesday, October 20, just a week before launch day the Dow Jones lost a quarter of its value, and £50 billion was wiped off the London Stock Exchange. Suddenly, all bets were off on BP. There was even a question about whether it would go ahead.

It duly did, but the promoters went very quiet. The merchant bank leading the issue, NM Rothschild, put out a statement after BP: "The issue has been undersubscribed." However, the prangsters could not be kept down. One fund manager commented after the BP flop: "The simplest way out for Nigel Lawson was to send for Keith Best (the MP who had been convicted for making multiple share applications), and make him a national hero."

The BP share price stayed steadfastly below the issue price despite the fact that the Kuwait Investment Office went on a buying spree. It seemed Lamont's words were prophetic – "it was not a **rich** man's hobby."